WRITING
Research, Theory, and Applications

STEPHEN D. KRASHEN
University of Southern California

PERGAMON INSTITUTE OF ENGLISH

a member of the Pergamon Group

Oxford · New York · Toronto · Sydney · Paris · Frankfurt

U.K.	Pergamon Press Ltd., Headington Hill Hall, Oxford OX3 0BW, England
U.S.A.	Pergamon Press Inc., Maxwell House, Fairview Park, Elmsford, New York 10523, U.S.A.
CANADA	Pergamon Press Canada Ltd., Suite 104, 150 Consumers Road, Willowdale, Ontario M2J 1P9, Canada
AUSTRALIA	Pergamon Press (Aust.) Pty. Ltd., P.O. Box 544, Potts Point, N.S.W. 2011, Australia
FRANCE	Pergamon Press SARL, 24 rue des Ecoles, 75240 Paris, Cedex 05, France
FEDERAL REPUBLIC OF GERMANY	Pergamon Press GmbH, Hammerweg 6, D-6242 Kronberg-Taunus, Federal Republic of Germany

First edition 1984

Library of Congress Cataloguing in Publication Data

Krashen, Stephen D.
Writing, research, theory, and applications.
(Language teaching methodology series)
Bibliography: p.
1. English language—Rhetoric—Study and teaching.
I. Title.   II. Series.
PE1404.K67 1984   808'.042'071   83-25778.

British Library Cataloguing in Publication Data

Krashen Stephen D.
Writing: research, theory and applications.
(Language teaching methodology series)
1. English language—Writing.
I. Title.   II. Series.
808'.042   PE1408

ISBN 0-08-031103-2

Printed in Great Britain by Redwood Burn Ltd., Trowbridge.

Contents

Introduction

Several years ago, my colleague Ed Finegan and I had a series of discussions with composition teachers at our university. Our goal was simply to inform ourselves about current approaches to teaching writing, to get some idea of the state of the art.

We considered these teachers to be among the most highly qualified. They were, for the most part, graduate students in USC's successful and prestigious Ph.D. programs in rhetoric and were experienced classroom writing teachers. We talked to 15 instructors and heard 15 different stories. Approaches ranged from the traditional "theme a week" method, based on a different "mode" each week, to the Garrison method, involving extensive student-teacher conferences. Some classes kept a journal, others did not. Some used the traditional freshman reader, some read *Newsweek*, one read *Zen and the Art of Motorcycle Maintenance*, and some did no reading. Some studied problem-solving techniques, some did literary criticism, some did extra vocabulary and grammar exercises.

When asked why they utilized the methods they did, our instructors' answers were based on rumour, fashion, or tradition. Sometimes they used a method or technique because a colleague was using it and had mentioned that it seemed to work. More commonly, our teachers admitted that they taught in the way they were themselves taught. In no case did any teacher say that his approach was even influenced by research or current theory, even though all of them were somewhat familiar with current research on writing.

There are two reasons, I think, for this state of affairs, why research and theory have had such little impact on teaching. First, previous attempts to apply research and theory to teaching writing have not been successful. The reason for this, I believe, is that we have attempted to apply the wrong research and inappropriate theories. Transformational grammar, for example, is a wonderful theory of language structure. It is not, however, a theory of language acquisition and is an inappropriate basis for writing methodology.

A second reason is that the relevant research has not been presented to teachers in a coherent way, that is, in the form of a theory. This is partly due to the fact that a great deal of important research and thinking on writing is new (although some research on writing, as we shall see, dates back many years). The reliability of several crucial research results has been established only recently, and these results have been presented to teachers only piecemeal, in the form of progress reports in journal papers.

It is difficult to apply individual research results to the writing class; they are only fully comprehensible and usable when put in the framework of a coherent theory; it is the theory that can be applied, not separate research results. Only a general theory can tell us how the parts fit together, whether results are contradictory or consistent with other results. If research tells us, for example, that both reading a lot and writing a lot increase writing proficiency, are these results in conflict? Only a theory that specifies what contribution reading and writing make can tell us.

Only a general theory can tell us what a method is doing, what contributions individual techniques make to the acquisition of writing competence and what aspects of a method are truly important. Does it matter if the teacher corrects errors between drafts or at the end? Should students write complete compositions in class or work on drafts? Only a theory can distinguish the distinctive features of a method from the irrelevant features; only a theory can tell us what is important and what is ritual.

My purpose here is to relate research in writing to pedagogy, to introduce teachers and writers to empirical research on writing. The organization of this monograph is straightforward. The first section reviews the research itself, and is organized around these questions:

1. Does reading help develop writing ability?
2. Does writing practice help develop writing ability?
3. Can writing be deliberately taught?
4. Do good writers go about the act of writing differently from poor writers?
5. Do good writers have different concerns in writing?

The second section attempts to draw some generalizations from the research that can be applied to writing pedagogy. It attempts, in other words, to present a coherent theory of the acquisition of writing ability that is consistent with the research discussed in the first section. Finally, the third section discusses applications of the theory to writing programmes.

One more comment before we begin. While my goal is clearly to propose a theory and relate theory to method, I do not think that theory should be the only determinant of method. Theory is always tentative; regardless of how much supporting evidence we have, a single convincing piece of counterevidence can destroy any hypothesis. But theory is useful—it attempts to summarize and draw general conclusions from many different observations. My hope is therefore that teachers of writing will consider the theory, not simply believe it, and relate the theory and research to their own experiences in writing and teaching writing. My hope is also that they will gain some understanding of the current state of research and theory and be encouraged to read and examine the professional literature on their own. It may not contain all the answers, but it will add the experience of others to their own experience and can provide writing teachers with additional insights and tools to help them in their difficult task.

What is known about Learning to Write

In this section, we briefly review research that supports what appears to be different and competing hypotheses concerning the development of writing ability. As we shall see in the second section of this monograph, it is possible to find deeper generalizations consistent with all the evidence presented here.

Reading and Writing

A variety of studies[1] indicate that voluntary pleasure reading contributes to the development of writing ability. Our study (Kimberling, Wingate, Rosser, DiChara and Krashen, cited in Krashen, 1978) examined this issue directly. Sixty-six USC freshmen were given a questionnaire and were asked to write an essay at home, which was evaluated by two raters. Only those essays judged to be "highly competent" and "of low competence" were retained for further analysis. The questionnaire asked students to indicate the amount of pleasure reading they had done at different times in their lives. We found very clear differences between good writers and poor writers—good writers reported more pleasure reading at all ages, and especially during the high school years. In fact, not one poor writer reported "a lot" of pleasure reading during high school.[2]

Woodward and Phillips (1967) surveyed 919 freshmen at the University of Miami. Good writers were defined as those who received grades of "A" or "B" in freshman writing, while poor writers received "D" or "E". Good writers reported more reading of the daily newspaper than poor writers (the only question that probed voluntary reading habits). There were no outstanding differences between the groups with respect to the amount of assigned reading done in high school, although more poor writers reported no assigned reading.

Applebee's survey (Applebee, 1978) of 481 good high school writers, winners of the 1967 NCTE achievement awards in writing, adds further evidence, although no control group was investigated. Applebee reported that ". . . these successful writers were also regulars readers. For voluntary reading, they reported an average of 14 books over the summer vacation, and another four books in their first eight to ten weeks of their senior year." (p. 340).

Donalson (1967) compared "effective" and "ineffective" tenth grade writers, writing quality in this case being determined by rating of three compositions by high school English teachers. Questionnaire results revealed that effective writers read "more widely and more frequently" (p. 40), reported more magazines in the home (C coefficient = .38) and owned more books (C = .23).

Ryan (1977) compared 54 "regular" and 55 "intensive" writers, that is, those in normal college freshmen writing classes and those who were assigned to special sections because of writing problems. After conducting home interviews, Ryan reported that the regular writers' homes had more books, and a greater variety of books. (This result is consistent with Donalson's finding of more magazines in the homes of effective tenth grade writers, but is only weakly supported by Woodward and Phillips, who found that more poor writers reported no books in the home; equal numbers of good and poor writers reported many books in the home, however.) Ryan also reported that the parents of good writers had read to them more as children, and that these parents also read more themselves.

McNeil (in Fader, 1976) evaluated the results of a pleasure reading programme ("Hooked on Books") on boys aged 12 to 17 in a correctional school in Michigan over a two year period. He reported that the "readers" showed significantly greater writing fluency and wrote with greater complexity than did control subjects. The readers also gained in self-esteem as compared to controls, were less anxious about school, improved in attitudes toward reading and writing, and were superior in reading comprehension.

One study apparently did not find a pleasure reading–writing relationship. Illo (1976) reports that correlations self-reported pleasure reading and freshman composition grades at Shippensburg State College seemed "weak and uncertain" (p. 134). Illo, however, does not provide more detail than this.

Several studies report statistically significant correlations between reading ability and writing ability (e.g. Grobe and Grobe, 1977,

Mathews, Larsen, and Butler, 1945, both studies using college freshmen; Zeman, 1969, using second and third grade children; Evanechk, Ollil, and Armstrong, 1974, using sixth graders). This kind of result is to be expected if pleasure reading contributes to both good reading ability (as supported by McNeil, cited above) and good writing.

TABLE ONE

Research on Reading and Writing

study	subjects	findings
Kimberling *et al*	college freshmen	good writers report more pleasure reading when younger
Woodward & Phillips	college freshmen	good writers read the newspaper more
Applebee	high school	NCTE winners do a great deal of pleasure reading
Donalson	high school	effective writers read more, own more books, report more magazines in the home
Ryan	college freshmen	good writers had more books in the home, were read to more
McNeil	age 12 to 17	boys who get "hooked on books" improve more in writing attitude
Illo	college freshmen	"weak and uncertain" correlations between outside reading and writing

In several cases, increased reading has been compared to other treatments. As we shall see below, increasing reading has generally been found to be more effective in producing gains in writing than increasing writing frequency (Heys, 1962; De Vries, 1970). In addition, replacing grammar study with increased reading has also been found to be beneficial (Clark, 1935; Adams, 1932).

Writing and Writing Frequency

Several studies have been done to determine whether practice in writing *per se* contributes to the development of writing ability. Some studies support this hypothesis, while others do not. In addition, when the effects of writing frequency are compared to the effects of increasing reading, research reveals that reading has a stronger influence on improving writing.

Two surveys indicated that better college freshman writers report more school-related writing in high school. Bamberg (1978) compared UCLA freshmen who placed into the regular freshman writing class with those who had to take remedial writing, and found that the regular students had done more expository writing in high school. McQueen, Murray, and Evans (1963) reported better performance on the University of Nevada placement examinations and better grades in freshman writing for those students coming from high schools that required more writing. Woodward and Phillips (1967) found that more poor writers reported doing no writing in high school English.

There is also some evidence indicating that better high school writers write more outside of school. Stallard (1974) found this to be the case, but also reported that good writers did not do significantly more diary or journal writing than average high school writers. Donalson (1967) reported that good tenth grade writers did more non-assigned writing in general (C = .29) and more letter writing (C = .34).

Wall and Petrovsky (1981) studied freshman writers at the University of Pittsburgh, who were placed into one of four sections of composition class depending on their performance on the Nelson–Denny test and a holistically scored essay. Placement was confirmed subsequently by the instructor on the basis of class performance. Result of a questionnaire administered to 248 students revealed that the least able writers wrote fairly frequently outside of school ("self-sponsored" writing, not including letters). Striking differences were found, however, with respect to the kind of writing done. The most advanced group reported the most variety of self-sponsored writing, while the lowest group showed "a lack of familiarity with anything other than expressive writing" (p. 119). In agreement with Bamberg and McQueen *et al.,* Wall and Petrovsky reported that the most advanced group had taken more composition courses in high school.

TABLE TWO

Research on Writing and Writing Frequency

study	subjects	finding
Bamberg	college freshmen	better writers did more expository writing in high school
McQueen *et al*	college freshmen	better writers' high schools required more writing
Woodward & Phillips	college freshmen	more poor writers did no writing in high school
Stallard	high school	good writers write more outside of school
Donalson	college freshmen	good writers write more outside of school; do more letter writing
Wall & Petrovsky	college freshmen	good writers do a greater variety of outside writing and took more composition courses
Lokke & Wykoff	college freshmen	two themes per week slightly better than one theme per week
Dressel *et al*	college freshmen	frequent writers and infrequent writers show similar gains (writing outside composition class)
Arnold	high school	no difference between frequent writers and infrequent writers (in English class)

Simply increasing academic writing frequency does not result in significantly increased proficiency. Very small effects for writing frequency and improvement in writing quality were found by Lokke and Wykoff (1948), who compared college freshmen at Purdue who wrote two themes per week in writing class with those who wrote one theme per week. The former group showed slightly higher grades in composition class at the end of the semester and their final compositions were rated slightly higher. Dressel, Schmid, and Kincaid (1952) compared college freshmen who were assigned a great deal of writing outside of class (average 131 hours over a year) with those who were assigned very little writing outside of writing class (average four hours over the year). Dressel *et al* reported that both groups improved their writing ability but no significant differences between the frequent and infrequent writers were found. Arnold (1964) compared tenth graders who wrote frequently in English class (at least once per week) with students who wrote infrequently (three times per semester). No differences in writing improvement were found at the end of the year.

Reading and Writing Compared

Three studies compare the effects of reading and writing on encouraging development of the writing skill. In each case, a group of students who wrote frequently was compared to a group that wrote less (and in one case, not at all) and spent more time reading.

In Heys (1962), subjects were high school students, grades nine to twelve. "Writing" classes wrote a theme a week, which was corrected "rigorously" by the teacher, while "reading" classes wrote a theme every third week and spent one period per week reading in class. At the end of the year, both groups showed clear progress, but the "reading" group outperformed the "writing" classes on the STEP writing test and received higher ratings on content and organization, mechanics, diction and rhetoric.

De Vries (1970) did a similar study with fifth graders. One group wrote two themes per week, while a second group did no writing, spending more time reading both in and out of class. Again, both groups gained in writing, with the reading group clearly outperforming the writing group on the post-test essay in all categories (content, mechanics, organization, grammar, wording and phrasing).

Christiansen (1965) compared two groups of college freshmen. One group wrote 24 themes during the semester and did no reading, while the second group wrote only eight themes and read prose selections from the freshman reader. Once again, both groups showed improvement, but no significant differences were found.

Thus, in two out of three cases, the reading group excelled, and in one case no difference was found. In no case did the frequent writers gain more than the readers.

TABLE THREE

Reading and Writing Compared

study	subjects	finding
Heys	high school	theme a week not as effective as theme every third week + reading
De Vries	grade 5	two themes per week not as effective as reading with no writing
Christiansen	college freshmen	8 themes per semester with reading as effective as 24 themes per semester

In summary, there is some evidence that practice in writing, especially expository writing, is related to improvement in writing ability. Not all studies report gains in writing ability with increased practice, however, and increased practice may not be as effective as increased reading.

Writing and Instruction

The research suggests that some aspects of the writing skill can be taught, but that there are limitations. The most general and obvious features of form and organization may be teachable. Bamberg's study, cited earlier, comparing "regular" and "remedial" college writers supports this generalization: the good writers not only did more expository writing in high school, they also had more instruction on aspects of form, such as supporting ideas with examples, clearly stating the topic or thesis of the essay, and paragraph structure. Shaughnessy (1977) studied "severely unprepared freshmen" and found that after one semester of "low intensity" instruction, almost all students showed improvement. Progress, however, was limited to the most obvious features. Students at the end of the course were able to "follow the rudiments of a plan . . . at least 50% of the students managed to stay with their topics. In illustrating their points, students tended to limit themselves to one example drawn usually from personal incident or observation and rarely did they choose to develop more than one aspect of a topic statement." (pp. 282–283).

Feedback

The research suggests that feedback is useful when it is done during the writing process, i.e. between drafts. It is not useful when done at the end, i.e. comments and corrections on papers read at home and returned to students. Beach (1979) found that teacher evaluation and correction of drafts had a positive effect on writing quality for high school students. Student self-evaluation did not improve writing, however. In addition, teacher evaluation only affected writing for one feature, the use of concrete examples. Simmons (1979) found that a conferencing approach, the Garrison method, produced significant gains for college writers. In the Garrison method, the teacher focuses only on one aspect of the students' writing at a time, beginning with having enough concrete information, then moving to aspects of organization, and finally to mechanics. Several drafts are required of the students, with teacher comment present at every intermediate stage.

Wall and Petrovsky (1981) found that their least able college freshmen writers reported having the most student–teacher conferences in high school (probably because of their obvious problems). Teacher comments to below-average writers tended to be limited to initial drafts; these students were thus left on their own to revise. The most advanced writers, on the other hand, reported more discussion that included final drafts in conferences with teachers. These results suggest that feedback encouraging and evaluating revision is more effective (see discussion of revision below).

Error correction limited to the final version of a composition, on the other hand, does not seem to help. Arnold (1964) compared the effect of full correction (every error marked by the teacher, corrected and rewritten by the student) to "moderate" correction (only one aspect at a time marked) in tenth grade students. No significant differences in writing ability were found at the end of the year. Stiff (1967) compared the effects of different kinds of comments on college freshmen papers (comments made in the margin, comments made at the conclusion, and both kinds together) and found no effect for any kind of feedback.

The effect of grammar instruction

The research strongly suggests that grammar instruction is not effective in helping students to write. Elley *et al* (1976) compared three groups of high school students in New Zealand: one group studied traditional grammar in English classes, a second studied transformational grammar, and a third studied no grammar. No differences in writing performance were found in their three year study. Bamberg, cited earlier, reported that good and poor freshman writers at UCLA did not differ with respect to the amount of grammar and mechanics they studied in high school English.

As mentioned earlier, increasing reading at the expense of grammar instruction has been found to result in more improvement in writing. Clark (1935) studied the effect of eliminating grammar drill and increasing reading in freshmen writing classes at the University of Illinois, and reported greater gains in essay writing, punctuation, spelling and grammar, with declines found in diction. Similar results were reported by Adams (1932): "boys who received instruction in literature over a period of 33 weeks wrote better and more accurate compositions than those instructed in grammar" (cited in Bagley, 1937, p. 143).

Correlations reported between tests of formal grammar and essay tests range from very low ($r = .18$; Hoyt, 1906, using grade school children; $r = .23$; Rapeer, 1913, for high school students) to modest ($r = .37$; Asker, 1923, for high school students.[3]

Research on the Composing Process

Studies show that good writers differ from poor writers in their composing processes, that is, they have better and more sound procedures for getting their ideas down on paper. Specifically, good writers differ in three ways: in planning, rescanning, and revising.

TABLE FOUR

Writing and Instruction

study	subjects	findings
Bamberg	college freshmen	good writers had more composition instruction than poor writers; no difference in amount of grammar, mechanics studied
Shaughnessy	college freshmen (remedial)	semester of instruction produces modest improvement in writing
Beach	college freshmen	teacher feedback between drafts more useful than student feedback (for concrete examples only)
Simmons	junior college freshmen	Garrison method produces better gains than traditional classes
Wall and Petrovsky	college freshmen	good writers had more conferences based on final drafts
Arnold	high school	"full" correction no better than "moderate" correction
Stiff	college freshmen	no effect for "marginal" "terminal" comments or both combined
Elley *et al*	high school	No difference in writing gains when traditional grammar, transformational, and no grammar study compared
Clark	college freshmen	dropping grammar and adding reading improves writing
Adams	elementary school	study of literature more beneficial than grammar study

Planning

The good writer plans more than the poor writer. This does not necessarily mean the use of a formal outline, nor is it always "prewriting". Emig's study (Emig, 1975) of professional writers revealed that very few used the standard outline form but all reported some kind of planning of content and organization before writing. Stallard (1974) found that good and average high school writers did not differ in outlining behaviour, but good writers took more time, regardless of whether they just thought or wrote notes, before actually writing, once they were given the topic in an in-class essay situation (4.18 minutes as compared to 1.2 minutes). Pianko (1979), in a study of "traditional" and "remedial" college freshmen reported similar results; as in Stallard's study, the better writers took more time before writing (1.64 minutes versus 1.0 minute) and reported doing more prewriting outside of school.[4] In both Stallard and Pianko's studies, few students reported using formal outlines.

Wall and Petrovsky (1981) found that more of their best freshman writers reported spending a long time thinking before beginning to write. The least able writers "only sometimes think a long time before beginning to write, and rarely make any written plans or notes, preferring to begin by 'just beginning'" (p. 119).

Interviews conducted by Rose (1980) and Sommers (1980) show that not only do good writers plan more, they also have more flexible plans—they are more willing to change their ideas as they write and to revise their outline as new ideas and arguments emerge.

Rescanning

The good writer pauses more during writing and rereads his text more. Stallard's good high school writers stopped to reread an average of 3.73 times per student during the writing of an essay, while rereading occurred less than once per student among the poor writers. Pianko's "traditional" students paused nearly twice as often during writing as remedial students and rescanned their work nearly three times as often (an average of 11.71 times per composition as compared to 3.7 times per composition).[5] Wall and Petrovsky also report a tendency for more frequent rereading among their more advanced writers, and Birdwell

(1980) reported that more successful twelfth grade writers reread first drafts before proceeding on to their second drafts.

Rescanning appears to help the good writers maintain a sense of the whole composition, or "conceptual blueprint" (Beach, 1979). Pianko notes that better writers, when they reread, "were pausing to plan what to write next, rescanning to see if their plans fit, and then pausing again to reformulate" (Pianko, 1979, p. 14).

What may be the case is that all writers have the problem of "losing their place", of losing a sense of the whole essay while in the act of writing. Good writers are aware of this problem and reread and rescan in order to review their overall plan and goals, consider improvements, and incorporate new ideas (see also Flower and Hayes, 1981; p. 382).

Revising

Some studies show that good writers revise more than poor writers do. Stallard found that his good high school writers averaged 12.24 revisions per paper as compared to 4.26 revisions per paper for average writers. More widely reported is the finding that writers revise differently, with better writers focusing on content and less able writers on surface form.

Sommers (1980) compared students and "experienced" writers (journalists, scholars, editors, etc.). Sommers reports that for the student writers, revision was basically rewording and adherence to school-learned rules. Student writers assumed that their desired meaning was present in their first draft; revision was simply a matter of finding the best words to express it. Sommers' experienced writers viewed revision differently; for them, revision was an effort to "find the line of the argument". The first draft may just be an attempt to "define their territory", while subsequent revisions help experienced writers continue to create meaning.

Faigley and Witte (1981) studied six professional writers, six advanced college writers (enrolled in upper division writing courses) and six inexperienced writers (college freshmen "deficient in writing skills"). Their subjects wrote on an assigned topic in three sessions, planning the first day and writing drafts on the second and third day. Faigley and Witte reported that the advanced college writers actually made the most revisions, but report startling differences between the groups with respect to revision type. As Sommers found, the more advanced writers made more content revisions, especially revisions that made a major difference in the meaning of the essay ("macrostructure" differences). Experienced writers made an average of 19.6 macrostructure changes per 1000 words of text, advanced writers made an average of 23.1 such changes, while inexperienced student writers made only 1.3 major changes per 1000 words of text. The expert writers made the fewest "meaning preserving" type changes, or paraphrases, and also made the fewest mechanical changes. Faigley and Witte also reported that the groups differed with respect to when they made changes, with the two more advanced groups delaying mechanical and word choice changes until the second draft, "cleaning up their manuscripts after they had satisfactorily dealt with their subjects. By this point inexperienced students had largely quit revising" (p. 409).

Wall and Petrovsky report similar results. Their best college freshman writers utilized revision more for invention, for adding changing content and for rearranging large sections of their compositions. As in Faigley and Witte's study, average writers actually did the most revision, but it was limited, for the most part, to the sentence level and was directed at clearer presentation of ideas present in the first draft—e.g. adding examples and rewording. Below average writers reported more second drafts than other groups, but in their case the second draft was often a completely new approach, a "second chance after a failed effort" (p. 118), not a revision. Wall and Petrovsky's least able group made the fewest word and phrase changes but were quite willing to add material.

Stallard reported that good high school writers were more concerned with word choice than average high school writers, while both groups showed equal concern with mechanics.

Perl (1979), in an intensive study of five "unskilled" college writers, also found that poor writers focus much more on form and less on content in revision. Perl also described how this practice can get in their way. One of her subjects, "Tony", for example, had a concern for correct form "that actually inhibited the development of ideas. In none of the writing sessions did he ever write more than two sentences before he began to edit" (p. 324). Of 234 changes Tony made in his composing sessions, over several compositions, only 24 had to do with content. The vast majority were changes in form, i.e. spelling, verb changes, etc.

Perl's five writers were apparently under the impression that revising was essentially editing, the application of conscious rules to small points of grammar, spelling and punctuation, and that such editing was a supremely important part of the composing process. Perl notes that their "premature" editing broke "the rhythm generated by thinking and writing", causing these writers "to lose track of their ideas" (p. 333). Sadly, this obsession with editing did not even result in more error-free writing for Tony; Perl found little improvement in mechanics in his later drafts.

We can summarize differences in revision as follows: Experienced writers focus on content in revision. Average college and high school writers use revision to clarify the meaning contained in the first draft. Below average writers are less concerned with clarification, and remedial writers confuse revision and editing, focusing on mechanics, grammar, and spelling.

Recursion

Research on the composing process also indicates that more successful writers do not always utilize a strictly linear plan—while some experienced writers actually plan first, write a draft, and then revise, in that order (see Selzer, 1983, for a description of the linear writing process of a technical writer), many good writers employ a recursive, non-linear approach—writing of a draft may be interrupted by more planning, and revision may lead to reformulation, with a great deal of recycling to earlier stages.

Sommers (1981) presents two interesting case histories illustrating this. Sommers' experienced writer, Walter, was willing to restart the plan-write-revise cycle all over again at any time, and many of the ideas found in his final version were not present in his first draft. While Walter began with a plan, he discovered much of the content of his essay while in the process of writing, discoveries that sent him back to replanning. Sommers' less experienced writer, Rita, was unable to do this because of her impression that she needed to follow certain school-taught rules. For her, the writing process consisted of taking an idea and pouring it into a predetermined mould: "What Rita assumed was that the meaning to be communicated was already there, already produced once she formulated her thesis statement, and all that she needed to do was follow a formulaic four or five paragraph essay form and stuff her 'meaning' into her paragraphs" (p. 48). This belief prevented her from discovering new ideas as she wrote.

TABLE FIVE

Research on the Writing Process

study	subjects	findings
Stallard	high school	good writers plan more
Pianko	college freshmen	
Wall & Petrovsky	college freshmen	
Stallard	high school	good writers reread, rescan more
Wall & Petrovksy	college freshmen	
Birdwell	high school	
Sommers	"experienced" and	experienced writers use revision for
Faigley & Witte	novice writers	invention, finding new ideas
Sommers	as above	novice writers use revision for
Stallard	high school	clarification; to find the "right words"
Perl	college freshmen	remedial writers confuse revision with
	(remedial)	editing, focus on mechanics, spelling
Sommers	as above	experienced writers willing to recycle,
		have "recursive" writing process

In summary, research on the composing process shows us that writing does not consist of simply creating an essay from start to finish in one smooth linear flow. It is, in Shaughnessy's words, a "messy process that leads to clarity" (p. 79). The good writer understands this, but the poor writer may not.

Awareness of Audience

Flower and Hayes (1980) report another difference between more and less capable writers. They examined, in detail, comments writers made as they composed, "thinking aloud" protocols of writers who "verbalized their thinking process as they wrote" (p. 23). Flower and Hayes found clear differences between "expert writers", teachers of writing with NEH fellowships to study writing, and "novice" writers, college freshmen diagnosed as having writing problems. The expert writers were far more concerned with their reader, their audience. They spent more time thinking about the effect they wanted to make on the reader, how they wanted to present themselves to the reader (what "voice" to use), what background knowledge the reader needed to have, what might interest the reader, etc. Novice writers, on the other hand, tended to be "tied to the topic" (p. 27) and spent less time thinking about the reader. A particularly vivid example was one novice writer, an engineering student, who, when asked to write about his job for readers of *Seventeen* magazine (13 to 15 year old girls), ended up with a "detailed technical analysis of steam turbulence in an electrical generator" (p. 30)!

Flower (1979) suggests that novice writers have difficulty in converting "writer-based prose" to "reader-based prose". All writers, she suggests, have access to writer-based prose, a personal style that "reflects the interior monologue of a writer thinking and talking to himself" (Flower, 1981, p. 63).[6] Use of writer-based prose may be quite useful as an initial step in getting out a first draft, but it does not communicate well to a reader: writer-based prose is characterized by ambiguous referents, words with special meanings to the writer that are not made precise to the reader, and a lack of a hierarchical organization, with main ideas and arguments clearly presented. Good writers, Flower maintains, convert writer-based prose to reader-based prose, a less egocentric style that attempts to be sensitive to the reader's needs. Less effective writers may be unaware of the reader's needs or they may be aware of them but unwilling or unable to consider them in writing.

Competence and Performance in Writing

The research results reviewed in the previous sections appear to support different and perhaps competing hypotheses. There is evidence, we have seen, that indicates that self-motivated reading relates to writing, some evidence that writing frequency relates to writing ability, that aspects of the writing skill can be deliberately taught, that formal grammar study does not contribute significantly to writing, and that good and poor writers have different composing processes and concerns. It is possible, however, to interpret the research as supporting a simple, coherent theory. The theory separates writing *competence*, or the abstract knowledge the proficient writer has about writing, from *performance,* the ability to put this knowledge to use in an actual piece of writing (these terms are from Chomsky, 1965).

Competence

Writing competence, it is hypothesized, comes only from large amounts of self-motivated reading for interest and/or pleasure. It is acquired subconsciously; readers are unaware they are acquiring writing competence while they are reading, and are unaware of this accomplishment after acquisition has taken place. It is reading that gives the writer the "feel" for the look and texture of reader-based prose.

This hypothesis is not new. In addition to my earlier statement (Krashen, 1978), Flower and Hayes (1980) and Smith (1983) have come to similar conclusions. Flower and Hayes note that good writers have a great deal of tacit knowledge of conventional or formal features of reader-based prose that they are able to call upon, more options that can be used to organize and express their ideas. They note "this may be one way in which extensive reading affects a person's ability to write: a well-read person simply has a much larger and richer set of images of what a text can look like" (p. 28).

Smith (1983) also maintains that the conventions of writing are acquired by reading: "To learn how to write for newspapers, you must read newspapers; textbooks about them will not suffice. For magazines, browse through magazines rather than through correspondence courses on magazine writing. To write poetry, read it. For the conventional style of memoranda in your school, consult your school file" (p. 560).

This hypothesis does not predict a perfect correlation between the amount of pleasure reading done and writing quality. It maintains only that all good writers will have done large amounts of pleasure reading, not simply "the more reading, the better the writing". There is, in other words, a minimum amount of reading that every good writer has done. The reading hypothesis thus does not distinguish excellent writers from merely good writers — other factors, such as creativity and experience, certainly play a role. Rather, good writers and excellent writers have both read "enough" to have acquired the code of written language.[7]

Second Language Acquisition and Learning to Write

The hypothesis that writing develops through reading accounts for the research on reading and writing reviewed in section one. It also suggests that competence in writing develops the same way competence in second languages develops. Second language acquisition theory distinguishes language *acquisition*, a subconscious process similar to child first language acquisition, from second language *learning*, a conscious process ("knowing about language"). Extensive research (reviewed in Krashen, 1981, 1982) has confirmed that acquisition is a far more powerful and central process than learning. Acquisition is responsible for our ability to use language in both production and comprehension, while conscious learning serves only as an editor or monitor, making changes in the form of output under certain, very limited conditions (i.e. when the performer knows the rule well, when the performer is consciously concerned with accuracy).

According to second language acquisition theory, we acquire in only one way — via comprehensible input. Acquisition does not happen by practising speaking or writing and getting feedback on the correctness of form.[8] It happens when we understand messages in the second language, when we understand *what* is said or written, rather than *how* it is expressed, when we focus on meaning and not form.

Speech is considered to be a result of language acquisition and not its cause. Speech emerges naturally after the acquirer has obtained a great deal of comprehensible input, and the grammatical accuracy of speech improves with more input. In fact, acquirers do best when they are not required to talk at all in early stages of second language acquisition, when they are allowed a silent period, a period during which they receive large amounts of comprehensible input via listening and reading. (Acquirers need not be forced to be silent in early stages; some people like to talk right away. The research indicates that early talk should not be required.)

I have argued (Krashen, 1982) that the "best" input for second language acquisition is not "grammatically sequenced", that is, does not focus on one aspect of grammar at a time (e.g. a lesson on the present tense, followed by a lesson on the past tense). While a predictable order of acquisition has been discovered by second language acquisition researchers (see Dulay, Burt and Krashen, 1982, for a review of this research), this does not mean we should teach language structure by structure along this order. When comprehensible input is supplied in enough variety and quantity, it is hypothesized that acquirers automatically receive far better exposure to and practise on those structures they are "ready" to acquire next, as compared to a grammatically sequenced approach.

Comprehensible input is necessary for second language acquisition, but it is not sufficient. In some cases, input is provided and understood, but does not result in acquisition. To account for this the Affective Filter hypothesis was formulated. This hypothesis claims that when affective conditions are not optimal, when the student is not motivated, does not identify with speakers of the second language, or is overanxious about his performance, a mental block, called the Affective Filter will prevent the input from reaching those parts of the brain responsible for language acquisition. It may be that for the Affective Filter to be completely "down", the acquirer's focus must be totally off the code and completely on the message: Acquisition may happen most efficiently when the acquirer "forgets" that he is listening to or reading another language.[9]

This theory implies that second language classes should be filled with comprehensible input presented in a low-anxiety situation. This is precisely what newer and more successful methods do, such as Terrell's *Natural Approach,* Asher's *Total Physical Response* method, and Lozanov's *Suggestopedia* method. The second language class is considered a very good place for beginning second language acquisition, since it can provide the comprehensible input that the "outside" world will not supply to older acquirers. The goal of the second language class is to bring acquirers to the point where they can begin to understand the language they hear and read outside of class and thus improve on their own.

Conscious rule-learning is not excluded from the second language program but it no longer has the central role. Students can apply conscious rules to their output when such "Monitor-use" does not interfere with communication — for most people, in writing and planned speech. Such Monitor-use can slightly but significantly raise the formal accuracy of output, but it appears to be the case that only a small percentage of the rules of a language are consciously learnable even by able adult students.

If second language acquisition and the development of writing ability occur in the same way, writing ability is not learned but is acquired via extensive reading in which the focus of the reader is on the message, i.e. reading for genuine interest and/or pleasure. Just as speech is hypothesized to be a result of comprehensible input, the ability to write is hypothesized to be a result of reading. Moreover, when enough reading is done, all the necessary grammatical structures and discourse rules for writing will automatically be presented to the writer in sufficient quantity. These rules and structures will be acquired if the reader is "open" to the input, if his Affective Filter is low. This occurs when the reader is completely focused on the message he is reading, and if his anxiety level is low (see below; "The Limits of Reading"). Rule learning, according to this view, has a limited role in both second language acquisition and in the development of writing ability. Conscious rules may be used to fill some of the gaps left by incomplete acquisition. Their use in speech in second language performance can seriously impede communication; similarly, their use in early stages of the composing process can interfere with the creation of meaning.

The Complexity Argument

There is considerable research supporting the validity of the input hypothesis for second language acquisition; as noted above, methods that emphasize comprehensible input are much more efficient in language teaching than traditional grammar and drill methods, for example (see Krashen, 1982, chapter five, for a review, and chapter one for other kinds of evidence). The enormous complexity of the grammar of any language is another powerful argument for the hypothesis that language competence must be acquired and that conscious learning can at best make only a small contribution. Linguists have described, by their own admission, only fragments of the grammar of the best described natural language, English, and language teachers know only a portion of this fragment. Moreover, teachers do not teach all they know about grammar and the best students do not learn all the rules presented. Finally, even the best students cannot remember and use all the rules they learn! Thus, only a small portion of the grammar of a language is available to the performer.

A very similar argument can be made concerning the learnability of the grammar and discourse structure of planned discourse, or good writing. We are now only beginning to discover the often subtle grammatical differences between good and poor writing (see e.g. Potter, 1970 and comments in Pringle, 1983). Descriptive studies, such as Crystal and Davy (1969), show how amazingly complex serious writing is, and how little our pedagogical descriptions capture. This predicts that explicit instruction in both grammar and organization will succeed only in teaching the most obvious and straightforward features of organization, a prediction that is quite consistent with the research cited earlier.

Smith (1983) makes the identical point, noting that the amount and complexity of language that must be acquired by the writer is "staggering", and could not possibly be learned one item at a time, by error correction, or by conscious rule. Using spelling as an example, Smith estimates that literate people know how to spell about 50,000 words. Smith concludes that spelling competence must come from reading, since spelling rules are too numerous, complex, and have too many exceptions to be consciously learned. In addition, it is highly doubtful that competent spellers received error-correction on all the words they know or looked each one up (see also Smith, 1981a, pp. 106–107, and Smith, 1982, pp. 161–162).

Similarly, "even arbitrary 'rules', descriptions, and definitions evade us when it comes to subtle matters as style, the intricate registers that depend on the topic of discussion and the audience addressed, and the 'schemas' appropriate to the particular medium being employed. Not only must letters, telegrams, formal and informal notes, newspaper reports, magazine articles, short stories, and poems be composed differently, the format of the genre itself varies depending upon its specific purpose. Letters to close friends and to the bank manager have no more in common than news items in the *National Enquirer* and in the *Wall Street Journal*. These conventions remain to be fully investigated by linguists, who have only recently begun to analyse many critical aspects of language which everyone observes and expects, in speech and in competent writing, without awareness of their existence . . ." (Smith, 1983, pp. 559–560).

If the student-writer is able to consciously learn all the rules of punctuation, spelling, grammar, and style that linguists have discovered and described, his reward should be a Ph.D. in linguistics. Unfortunately, this will not guarantee him writing competence, since so much of what good writers do routinely and subconsciously remains to be discovered.[10]

The Limits of Reading

Just as comprehensible input is necessary for second language acquisition, but is not sufficient, reading is necessary but not sufficient for acquisition of writing competence. As Smith has noted, all readers do not necessarily become good writers. Smith argues that for a reader to acquire a writer's code, at least two factors must be present in addition to reading. The first condition is the expectation of success, or rather, "the absence of any expectation that learning (acquisition in my terms) will not take place or that it will be difficult" (Smith, 1981a, p. 111). Where learning (acquisition) is taken for granted, notes Smith, "we continue to learn throughout our lives" (p. 111). Second, Smith argues that the reader must consider himself to be a member of the same group or "club" as the writer, or at least a potential member. When an acquirer considers himself a member of the group, as writers or future writers, acquisition occurs without the necessity of external force; readers will write the way good writers do, just as "children never want to speak an inadequate version of the language of the groups to which they adhere, any more than they want to dress in a less than conventional way. If they are members of a club, they want to live to its standards" (Smith, 1983, p. 567). On the other hand, "the consequence of not being a member of the club is dramatic, for children and for adults. We do not learn. In effect, the brain learns not to learn, it shuts down its own sensitivity . . . exclusion from any club of learners is a condition difficult to reverse, whether we impose it on ourselves or have it imposed on us" (p. 562).

Smith's interpretation is, I think, fully compatible with the Affective Filter hypothesis for second language acquisition. The existence of an Affective Filter, as discussed above, was hypothesized to explain why acquisition sometimes stops short, even where comprehensible input is available in sufficient quantity, and why acquirers choose one dialect over another (Dulay and Burt, 1977). The components of the Affective Filter derive from second language acquisition research relating certain affective variables and success in second language acquisition, including "integrative motivation", the desire to be like members of the group speaking the second language (Gardner and Lambert, 1972), self-esteem, and anxiety level (correlations between anxiety level and success in second language acquisition are typically negative; the lower the anxiety, the better the acquisition). The conditions that result in a "low" Affective Filter (discussed in detail in Krashen, 1981) are quite similar to the conditions hypothesized by Smith to be relevant to the acquisition of writing competence. When success is assured, when anxiety about acquisition is low or non-existent, the filter is "low". When there is anxiety about acquisition, and/or when the acquirer feels excluded from the "club" of target language speakers, the filter is high, the brain "learns not to learn and shuts down its sensitivity".

Performance

If writing competence develops as a result of pleasure reading, then writing practice *per se* does not develop competence. We can explain the research results relating writing frequency and practice to ability by hypothesizing that writing practice helps *performance*: Practice in writing, especially expository writing, helps writers discover an efficient composing process. Sheer practice, via trial and error, helps many writers understand the necessity of planning, rereading, and revision and helps them develop sound planning and revision strategies. The value of instruction is that it can help writers develop good strategies for performance more quickly and can help cure and prevent inefficient or "tangled" composing processes. According to this theory, however, writing practice and instruction will not help the writer actually acquire the code: This happens only via comprehensible input, reading. Conscious knowledge of rules of grammar and usage helps only at the editing stage and is limited to straightforward, learnable aspects of grammar.

Once again, Smith (1983) presents a similar argument. Instruction, according to Smith, should teach writers those aspects of writing that cannot be obtained from reading. Among other things, it should provide "knowledge of technicalities which a text cannot offer. Such technicalities range from the use of paper clips, index cards, and wastepaper baskets to the nature and utility of drafts and editing, none of which is apparent in published texts and none of which, therefore, the author can demonstrate" (p. 564). Writing practice cannot be the way writers gain competence, acquire knowledge of the code. As Smith notes: "I thought the answer (to how we learn to write) must be that we learn to write by writing until I reflected upon how little anyone writes in school, even the eager students, and how little feedback is provided. Errors may be corrected, but how often are correct models provided, especially beyond the level of words? How often is such feedback consulted, and acted upon, especially by those who need correction most? No one writes enough to learn more than a small part of what writers have to know . . ." (Smith, 1983, p. 560).

Summary

To summarize, the competence/performance theory outlined in this section accounts for the research findings in these ways: As is the case with oral language acquisition, competence in writing does not come from the study of form directly—the rules that describe written language, or "reader-based prose", are simply too complex and numerous to be explicitly taught and consciously learned. We gain competence in writing the same way we gain competence in oral language; by understanding messages encoded in written language, by reading for meaning. In this way, we gain a subconscious "feel" for written language, we acquire this code as a second dialect.

This hypothesis accounts for the research showing a relationship between pleasure reading and writing ability—better writers have acquired the written dialect via reading. It also accounts for the lack of a relationship shown between grammar study and writing ability and the modest effect of deliberate instruction on organization.

Cases in which sufficient reading has been done, but competence has not been developed, can be explained in terms of the Affective Filter. When the Filter is up, when readers are anxious, do not feel a part of the writer's world, they may understand what they read, but the input will not reach those parts of the brain that do language acquisition.

Writing competence is necessary, but is not sufficient. Writers who are competent, who have acquired the code, may still be unable to display their competence because of inefficient composing processes. Efficient composing processes, writing "performance", can be developed via sheer practice as well as instruction. This part of the theory explains the relationship between writing frequency and proficiency as well as the finding that good writers have often had more instruction in writing (more classes); these experiences, the theory predicts, did not result in acquisition of writing style; this can only be developed via reading. Rather, writing practice, whether in self-sponsored writing or in classes, can help writers develop efficient composing processes.

Applications: Solving Writing Problems

Writing Problems

The theory presented in the previous section makes predictions about the problems writers have, and also makes predictions about their solutions. Writers can have the following kinds of problems:
1. Lack of acquisition of the code (written English).
2. A poor or inefficient composing process.

We can define the *remedial* writer as one who has neither acquired the code nor has developed an efficient writing process. A *blocked* writer is one who has acquired the code but who has problems in performance. This classification is illustrated in table six.

TABLE SIX
A typology of writing problems

	competence	performance
remedial writer	−	−
blocked writer	+	−

If this analysis is correct, solving writing problems requires either or both of the following: Helping writers acquire the code and helping them develop an efficient composing process.

Acquiring the Code: Getting Hooked on Books

The theory implies that a central task for any language arts programme is getting students hooked on books. There is clear evidence that this responsibility is indeed recognized by many school districts and individual schools—many of Fader's suggestions in *Hooked on Books* have been followed—attractive book displays, more time devoted to reading, including sustained silent reading programmes, increased use of paperbacks, etc. The expense of books, even paperbacks, and the reduction of public library services and hours, place an increased burden on the school, on the language arts teacher, and on the school library. The theory and research clearly imply, however, that an investment in encouraging pleasure reading, certainly a modest one when compared to expensive educational technology, will pay off in better writing.

It may not, however, pay off immediately. While some of the studies cited earlier report clear increases in writing ability after relatively short periods of reading (e.g. Heys, 1962; De Vries, 1970; Clark, 1935) other studies suggest that good writing is a long-term payoff of reading (e.g. Ryan, 1977; Kimberling et al., 1978). One doesn't simply assign a few articles or even books and see immediate results—just as is the case in second language acquisition, large amounts of comprehensible input may be necessary before acquisition becomes evident. Thus, the teacher who succeeds in getting a student hooked on books may not see the results; next year's teacher may get the credit.

Theory gives us some reason for optimism on the writing potential of the "adult beginner". Despite our finding (Kimberling et al.) that the strongest relationship between reading and writing was found for reading done during the adolescent years, theory gives us no reason to conclude that a rigid "critical period" exists for the acquisition of the written language. Second language acquisition theory posits that acquisition via comprehensible input is possible at any age, and the same may very well be true of writing. While we do not have, as yet, long term longitudinal studies of adult beginners, our experience in second language acquisition is encouraging: Adults do attain high levels of proficiency in second languages, acquiring nearly all of the language, given adequate comprehensible input. It is thus very possible that remedial writers, even "adult beginners", will do just as well in learning to write.

Thus, the teacher's responsibility is to provide access to reading. To ensure a low affective filter, to assure that the student will expect success and expect to be a member of the "writer's club", teachers must also "show the advantages that membership of the club of writers offers and help students join" (Smith, 1983, p. 564). This entails showing students that writing is "interesting, possible, and worthwhile" (Smith, p. 566) via writing activities that are natural and genuine. According to the theory, efforts in this direction will help ensure that the language the student reads will become acquired and available for his use in writing.

Developing an Efficient Composing Process

Delaying editing and using writer-based prose

As table six indicates, both readers and non-readers may have inefficient writing processes. A major problem for non-readers in writing performance is the fact that they have not acquired the code; they do not have a feel for what good writing looks like. In many cases, however, they have been exposed to years of grammar teaching. The result is that they use, and often over-use, these conscious rules in writing, as Perl's research shows. Perhaps our goal here should be to help the non-reader separate revision from editing, encouraging students to do as Faigley and Witte's advanced writers did, attending to only content revisions at first, and delaying editing changes until the last draft. Editing should also be limited to those parts of the grammar that are "learnable", concrete rules that can be described in a straight-forward way and remembered. We should wait for acquisition to deal with the subtle and complex areas of syntax and organization. These practices may reduce the over-editing many poor writers do and increase fluency. (See also Smith, 1982, for a similar suggestion. Smith recommends separating "composition" from "transcription", because they make very different kinds of demands on the writer's attention. Premature concern with transcription, according to Smith, is "as pointless as gift-wrapping the package before the contents have been put inside" (p. 184).)

Flower (1979, 1981) pushes the idea of delaying editing further and suggests that it is often useful for writers to attempt only to produce writer-based prose at first, ignoring the reader in initial efforts. According to Flower, this approach "allows the writer freedom to generate a breadth of information and a variety of alternative relationships before locking himself or herself into a premature formulation" (Flower, 1979, p. 36). Starting with writer-based prose lowers the cognitive load, delaying many formal considerations while the writer works out his ideas.

This step needs to be followed by the transformation of writer-based prose to reader-based prose, prose that takes the reader into account, as Flower notes. This entails selecting a focus of mutual interest, moving from facts and details to concepts, and changing narrative or episodic style into expository style organized around the writer's purpose (Flower, 1979, p. 37).[11] The transformation from writer to reader-based prose can happen at any "stage" in the writing process: "When it goes on in our heads before we commit words to paper, we call it thinking and organizing. When we do it slightly later and on paper, we call it revision. The critical skill here is being able to organize what one knows with a reader in mind. It is this basic thinking process which counts, not the point at which the writer performs it" (Flower, 1981, p. 72). The writer who has read has subconsciously acquired the formal features of reader-based prose; for these writers, part of this transformation involves simply switching from one subconsciously acquired dialect to another.

Superstitions

Both remedial writers and blocked writers may believe in superstitions about writing that inhibit their writing performance. Rose (1980) discusses several interesting examples. One college student, Laura, was told in both high school and college English classes that every essay had to include at least three points. This belief forced Laura to include irrelevant material in her writing. Another student, Martha, felt that the outline had to include every possible detail and produced outlines of tremendous complexity. According to Rose, this practice "locked her into the first stage of the composing process" (p. 394); Martha could not convert her overly detailed plan into a short paper.

A third case described by Rose, Ruth, was told in English class that "a good essay always grabs a reader's attention immediately" (p. 394). While good introductions are undoubtedly very helpful, Ruth was under the impression that if she could not come up with a sensational introduction for her compositions, she could not go on writing; "for Ruth, this means that beginning bland and seeing what emerges as one generates prose is unacceptable" (p. 394). The result was immobilization.

As noted earlier, good writers often get important ideas while in the process of writing. Over-adherence to learned rules of form may prevent writers from concerning themselves with meaning and from discovering new ideas while writing (Sommers, 1981).

Perhaps the most pervasive and most dangerous false belief some writers have is that there is no writing process, that experienced writers simply sit down at the typewriter, begin at the beginning, and write through to the end, with no planning, revision, or break in the linear flow. As Shaughnessy points out, many students have the mistaken impression that "the point in writing is to get everything right the first time and that the need to change things is a mark of the amateur . . . Indeed, beginning writers often blame themselves for having to revise and even for not being able to start at all—problems only too familiar to the professional writer as well" (pp. 79, 81). Students get this impression perhaps because they only see the written product and never witness demonstrations of planning and revision (Smith, 1983, p. 196). The fact that good writers plan and revise, and produce many drafts is "one of the best kept secrets in school" (Smith, 1982, p. 1960).

We further encourage this error when we assign compositions in class and require students to finish within the hour. Such assignments convince students that extensive planning is not necessary or desirable (recall Stallard's and Pianko's findings of extremely brief planning periods for in-class writing, discussed earlier), and that revision is not part of the writing process, since there is simply not enough time to do more than write a single draft. In-class writing can be very profitable, but it gives the wrong impression when we expect students to start and finish an essay in an hour.[12]

Practice

The theory and research suggest that pedagogy aimed at improving student composing processes should include a fair amount of sheer practice in writing. This practice would help students discover not only the universal elements of efficient composing processes, but also to help them choose among different options available to them, e.g. what sort of planning to use, a traditional outline, clustering, the use of writer-based prose, etc. It might also be helpful to show students examples of how good writers compose, both to provide some options as well as to dispel the myth that there is no composing process. Both theory and research indicate that conferencing techniques, such as the Garrison method, will be effective; they give direct and clear practice in working through the composing process.

Advice

Finally, some explicit advice may be helpful. The following short list attempts to summarize the major findings of the research on the composing process for presentation to students:

1. Have at least a rough outline or plan before you begin to write. Be prepared to change your outline as you write and as your ideas develop.
2. Don't over-edit early drafts. A draft is just a draft. Delay consideration of mechanics, spelling and punctuation until you are satisfied with the content of your paper.
3. Keep the whole composition in mind as you write. It is very easy to lose your place. Occasionally stop and consider what you have read to remind yourself of the overall organization.

(In my own writing class at the college level, students not only received this information, but read some of the research reports cited and described here. This had several advantages—it provided us with a topic, something to discuss and write about, and provided explanation and empirical justification for some of my teaching practices that differed from what their previous writing and English teachers had done, e.g. why we used conferencing techniques, why I reacted to drafts and did not simply correct and hand back finished products, why we did not write complete essays in one class period, etc. Several of the less technical articles cited here are quite readable by students at this level, e.g. Sommers, 1980; Heys, 1962; Smith, 1983).

The Role of Grammar Teaching

The theory presented here does not imply that grammar teaching must be dropped from language arts; it does, however, force a re-evaluation of its role. Grammar teaching has two possible functions in the language arts programme. First, grammar has a role to play in what should be the final stage of the composing process, editing. Writers can use their conscious knowledge of grammar to fill in the gaps left by acquisition, to supply those grammatical items and bits of punctuation that reading has not provided. Even widely read writers may have a "residue", a small set of conventions and rules that acquisition has not provided. These items can and should be taught; their absence gives writing an unpolished and uneducated look. What is crucial, however, is that this aspect of the language arts programme not be allowed to dominate; it is a small part of teaching students to write. As we have seen in our discussion of Perl's research, overteaching of grammar for editing can seriously impair the composing process.

Which rules should be taught for this purpose? My impression is that many teachers and handbooks emphasize these rules now. Items such as the "loose-lose" contrast, the "it's–its" distinction, and the "there–their–they're" set may require appeal to conscious rules even among well-read writers. Again, what is important is that it be recognized that teaching these items, while necessary, is a small part of language arts. Such teaching and error-correction should be limited to straightforward rules and their application should be limited to editing, the very last stage of the composing process.[13,14]

A second function for grammar teaching has nothing to do with developing writing ability. It is providing students with information about the structure of language, known as linguistics. The sentence diagramming exercises prominent in some programmes have, I think, this implicit goal. There are many educational benefits deriving from the study of linguistics. The study of the structure of language gives students an appreciation of surface differences and deep similarities among the languages of the world and their speakers. This leads to discussion of language universals, and Chomsky's hypothesis that universally found structures are innate. Linguistics includes the study of historical linguistics and sociolinguistics, with their implications for "non-standard" dialects, prescriptivism and correctness in usage. It also includes the study of language acquisition in children and adults. This worthy area of inquiry, however, is subject matter, like geography or math. It needs to be distinguished from teaching students to write.

A similar argument can be made for teaching students about the structure of written discourse. Readers don't need these rules to improve their writing: instructions from the teacher on how to write, rules on the use of topic sentences, transitions, conclusions, etc., are in a sense old information for those who have read, as they have already acquired these concepts subconsciously. Moreover, insisting that students closely follow certain rhetorical models can have the effect of preventing them from discovering meaning as they write (recall the case of Sommers' student Rita, discussed earlier). But there is educational value in learning about the structure of prose. Societies show both similarities and differences in how they organize their writing (Kaplan, 1972), and this information may deepen understanding of different cultures and explain some kinds of miscommunication.

Conclusions

The competence/performance theory, constructed to account for the research findings in section one, implies that instruction in writing should not focus on teaching form directly, but should instead encourage the subconscious acquisition of form through reading and give students procedures that will facilitate the discovery of meaning and an efficient writing process. There are several reasons why we may be tempted to teach form directly, to give students rules for organization and grammar. First, it has often been argued that in some cases, we cannot wait for acquisition; the remedial writer is in a hurry—he has a test to pass, or other subject matter teachers to satisfy. He therefore needs some formulae, some rules for a "quick fix", a band-aid to get him through until acquisition can do its job.

According to the theory and research presented here, this is an invalid argument. At best, providing these students with more information about the product will result in a wooden, awkward approximation to good prose. At worst, it can seriously inhibit their writing processes. As Sommers' and Perl's case histories show, overteaching can prevent the discovery of new meaning and can seriously disrupt fluency and the flow of ideas onto the page. Moreover, when traditional instruction and reading have been compared in the research, students undergoing the reading treatment have done better (Clark, 1935). Remedial writers are probably the most in need of reading and writing for meaning, and the most damaged by excessive rule teaching.

I suspect that another reason we are drawn toward deliberate instruction is the excitement new discoveries in grammar and discourse analysis cause in some of us. Scholars and teachers, those interested in the structure of language for its own sake, take great pleasure in learning something they have already acquired, in discovering a rule that describes what we previously knew only tacitly. It seems obvious to many of us that this new information must be of use to our students, that if we simply tell them about the new rule, and provide them with some practice in using it in writing, that it will become automatic, and part of their permanent repertoire. But learning does not turn into acquisition: many fine writers have never consciously learned the rules for composition, and many people who have learned even valid rules and who have practised them assiduously cannot use them. According to the theory, the acquisition of language occurs in only one way, via comprehensible input. The acquisition of the special dialect known as the written language also occurs in only one way—via comprehensible input of messages encoded in that dialect, known as reading. Conscious knowledge is not a prerequisite for acquisition. It can, in fact, be a detriment if misused.

Our students are therefore not dependent on the results of linguistic science to learn to write, and an effective writing teacher need not be a linguist or discourse analyst. You need not know the code consciously to teach it, just as parents do not need to master transformational-generative grammar to help their children acquire language. Development of good writing style occurs via reading for meaning and writing to convey meaning. It has happened this way to millions of people, and there seems to be no way to shortcut the process.

Our pedagogical efforts, it seems to me, should be directed towards finding ways of taking advantage of our innate ability to acquire language. There is no reason to try to accelerate or replace this natural process: It is efficient, rapid enough when input is provided, less expensive than its substitutes, and by far less tedious.

Appendix: Writing in a Second Language

Despite the existence of large numbers of published texts on second language writing, and the existence of many programs, very little is known about writing in a second language. While reasonable suggestions have been made on the basis of first language research (e.g. Taylor, 1981; Zamel, 1981), empirical investigation is lacking. The data that does exist, however, shows clear similarities with first language writing, suggesting that a similar competence/performance theory might be applicable and that significant similarities in pedagogical application are called for.

What is known about Second Language Writing

Reading and Writing

Given the relationship between reading and writing in first language, one might expect a similar relationship to hold between reading and writing in a second language. There is, however, no published evidence relating reading and writing proficiency in second language acquirers. A great deal of research indicates that comprehensible input is the cause of overall second language proficiency (Krashen, 1982), but in no case is mastery of "reader-based prose" used as a dependent variable.

A related question is the relationship between first language reading and second language writing. Despite differences in writing styles across cultures (Kaplan, 1972), there are also clear similarities; readers in any language might be expected to have acquired a feeling for reader-based prose in general. As Cummins (1981) has argued, the ability to use language in decontextualized situations appears to be learnable in any language and this ability can be applied to any other language.[15]

Writing and Writing Frequency

The only research I know of relating to the question of whether writing frequency and second language writing ability are related is Brière (1966), who found improvement in university level ESL students in a composition course that emphasized quantity of writing. Brière's measures, however, were fluency and grammatical accuracy, not evaluation of writing style.[16] No studies investigate whether frequent writing improves second language writing at levels higher than the sentence.

Instruction

There is research pertaining to the question of whether instruction helps second language acquisition in general. I have reviewed this research in Krashen (1982; pp. 33–37), and conclude that language teaching does in fact help second language acquisition when it is the major source of "comprehensible input". Intermediate and advanced students who have another source of comprehensible input available to them do not profit significantly from additional formal language classes, but beginners do profit from the language class. For beginners, the class can be a very good place to get the input needed for acquisition, while the "outside world" is not always as co-operative. Thus, instruction works when it provides comprehensible input, a hypothesis confirmed by method comparison research that shows that methods providing more comprehensible input and attempting to lower the affective filter produce much better results than traditional grammar and drill methods (Krashen, 1982; chapter five). None of these studies, however, deals directly with writing.

Similarly, there is a fair amount of evidence that error correction is not effective in second language acquisition (for a review, see Dulay, Burt and Krashen, 1982, pp. 35–36). Once again, however, the research has been focused exclusively on aspects of sentence-level grammar, morphology and pronunciation, and has not been concerned with writing quality.

The Composing Process in Second Language Writers

Zamel (1983) has filled the research gap here with a recent study of six advanced ESL students studying in an American university. Her subjects, students in her composition class, spoke different first languages (Chinese, Spanish, Portuguese, Hebrew, and Persian), and were observed while writing course-related assignments in an untimed task. This observational data was supplemented with interviews. On the basis of holistic ratings of pre- and post-course essays, four writers were categorized as "skilled" and two as "unskilled". The results of Zamel's study are remarkably similar to those found in first language writing.

Planning

Zamel reports that all students spent time thinking about the essay before writing. While some students actually wrote while planning, others did not, but no clear relationship was found between writing skill and writing while planning. One unskilled writer was disturbed by her inability to form a complete plan before writing, her feeling being that a complete outline was necessary. Zamel notes that "she . . . seemed to view writing as a straightforward expansion of such a plan" (p. 176) and while in the process of writing actually asked her teacher (Zamel) "Can I add something later?". Zamel's good writers did not have this attitude and seemed to know that they could "leave half-finished thoughts and come back to them later" (p. 176). Thus, in second language as well as first language, good writers have more flexible plans.

Revision

Zamel reports very clear differences between skilled and unskilled second language writers in revision behaviour. Skilled writers revised at all levels, from small points of form to important changes in content. Their attitudes toward revision were identical to those of experienced first language writers, as reported in Sommers (1980); they regarded revision as a means of discovering ideas. Here are some quotes:

"Unless you write about something, you can't find out exactly what you know about it."

"I don't even know what I'm thinking sometimes, but I'm finding out by writing." (p. 176).

Zamel's less skilled writers were mostly concerned with "local problems from the very beginning, changing words and phrases but rarely making changes that affected meaning" (p. 174). In fact, second and third drafts for one unskilled writer were simply "neater copies of her original". As was the case with Perl's subject Tony, this overconcern with form inhibited composing; Zamel's least skilled writer was so concerned with small points and paused so often, "that the overall relationship between ideas seemed to suffer" (p. 173).

Second Language Problems

Interestingly, Zamel's students did not regard the fact that they were writing in an as yet imperfectly acquired language as a serious problem. As one of them stated, "most of the difficulty is how to put the ideas together" (p. 179). While all the completed compositions had grammatical flaws, the more skilled writers delayed consideration of lexical and grammatical problems until the final stages of their writing—they did not let their second language weaknesses tangle their composing process. On the other hand, the least skilled writer "was determined not to commit errors and therefore attended to them prematurely" (p. 178), resulting in her losing track of her ideas. The better writers seemed to know that considering both form and content at the same time is difficult: "If I worry about grammar, my thoughts will disappear" (p. 173).

Conclusions

While studies of second language writing are sadly lacking, there is good reason to suspect that deep similarities exist between first and second language competence and performance, and that similar pedagogies are called for—reading for the acquisition of the written language, and writing practice for the development of an efficient composing process. There is every reason to expect that second language students will also profit from conferencing methods that guide them through the writing process and heighten awareness of audience. Similarly, the advice proposed for first language writers will also fit for second language writers, with, as we shall see, some additional advice to delay problems of grammar and vocabulary until the end.

With this deep similarity are surface differences, however. Second language writers will, of course, make more errors in grammar and lexical choice than will first language writers. Our temptation, on seeing these errors, is to correct them and to teach the correct form. Research in second language acquisition indicates, however, that this approach is very limited; only certain rules can be taught, and studies show that even proficient second language performers are able to correct only a small percentage of their own errors (Krashen, 1982, chapter four). According to theory, true acquisition of grammar can only come with comprehensible input; the use of conscious rules, even if successful, is only a temporary cure. This is not to imply that conscious learning of grammar is useless; there is no reason not to teach simple, straight-forward, "learnable" rules as long as the performer does not misuse them, that is, as long as they do not interfere with the composing process. Good "Monitor-users" will be able to raise the accuracy of their written output a modest but significant amount by the judicious use of conscious rules. The best way to apply these rules is to follow the procedure of Zamel's skilled writers: delay them until the end so that their application will not interfere with the flow of ideas.

Some second language errors are "developmental", that is, they are similar to the errors all language acquirers make *en route* to full acquisition. Other errors show the influence of the first language. Along with Newmark (1966), I have hypothesized (Krashen, 1981, 1982) that errors reflecting the structure of the first language are not the result of interference of first language habits but are simply the result of the performer's "falling back" on the first language in instances where second language competence was lacking. Use of first language patterns is thus a performance strategy that decreases as second language acquisition occurs. According to this view, we do not need special exercises that drill the student on just those points where the first and second languages are different—we simply need to encourage second language acquisition.

As noted earlier, some organizational features of first language writing do appear in the writing of second language student writers (Kaplan, 1972). Overconcern with these differences in pedagogy is not called for, however, since, as we have seen, such an emphasis on form may prevent the discovery of ideas in writing, and these features will disappear as second language acquisition occurs. As noted earlier, the study of similarities and differences has educational value for all language students, first and second, but is part of linguistics, not learning to write.

---

[1] Studies cited in this paper, in most cases, are published in standard scholarly sources. I have not included research that appears only in dissertations or in abstract form.

[2] The definition of "good writing" and "poor writing" varies from study to study, including grades in composition classes, ratings of essays, results of local and standardized tests of writing, syntactic maturity and teacher impression. Despite this variation, there is considerable consistency in findings.

[3] Mavrogenes and Padak (1982) investigated the effect of reading while listening with remedial ninth graders (students who tested below the fifth grade level in standardized tests of reading comprehension and vocabulary). Students read texts that were "well above" their reading level and that were selected for their potential interest while listening to a recording of the text. Teachers reported that students enjoyed the experience, and test results after 24 weeks showed significant gains in writing complexity (significantly more T-units used in a free writing assignment, as compared to controls). Another group that combined reading/listening with syntactic manipulation exercises also showed gains, but not as great as the reading/listening only group. Those who underwent only the syntactic manipulation treatment declined slightly on this measure. All three experimental groups showed gains on a sentence-combining task, with the reading/listening only group making the least gains.

[4] Apparent differences in planning time between the Stallard and Pianko studies may be due to the different levels of writing ability involved. The following table confirms that planning time increases with writing level and suggests that Stallard's and Pianko's categorizations are valid:

planning time:

	good writers	"average"	poor writers
Stallard (high school)	4.2″	1.2″	
Pianko (college freshmen)		1.64″	1.0″

The reader may also note how short planning time was in these studies; even good writers took only four minutes! This is undoubtedly due to the nature of the writing assignment (in-class in both cases). While I know of no research on this issue, it is evident that experienced writers take much longer, i.e. days, weeks, months, and (as in the case of this monograph) even years.

[5] Quantitative differences between Stallard's and Pianko's results are probably due to different definitions of rereading and rescanning. In each case, however, better writers engaged in more reviewing of their own writing.

[6] Elinor Ochs Keenan makes a similar distinction, positing the existence of "unplanned discourse" and "planned d)scourse" (Ochs Keenan, 1977). Ochs notes that both styles are available to the performer.

[7] The reading hypothesis predicts that there will be clear differences between "writers" (good and excellent) and "non-writers" (bad and horrible). This may explain the phenomenon noted in footnote two; regardless of the measure of writing used, studies of good and poor writers reviewed in section one show similar results.

[8] Error correction, according to the theory, affects only conscious learning, not acquisition. Error correction helps the learner adjust his conscious mental representation of the rule. As in the case in writing, research has failed to confirm that error correction has a significant impact on second language acquisition (see Dulay, Burt and Krashen, 1982, for a review).

[9] I have suggested (Krashen, 1982) that the reason adults do not, in general, attain the native speaker level of competence in second languages is because of an increased Affective Filter. The language acquisition device, I hypothesize, remains active and efficient throughout life. The impact of the filter is not overwhelming; it prevents only the last few inches of a mile-long journey—adults can and do acquire a great deal of second language ability. The filter is not the only reason many acquirers do not achieve native-speaker competence in second languages; it is not the only cause of "fossilization". Other causes include insufficient quantity or quality of input and the acquisition of imperfect forms of the target language. For further discussion, see Krashen and Terrell (1983) and Krashen (forthcoming).

[10] The "reading hypothesis" also provides an explanation for Ryan's finding of a relationship between reading to children and later writing success. One or both of the following may be true: in being read to, children discover that books can be interesting, and get "hooked"—the grade school teacher reads parts of E. B. White's *Charlotte's Web* in class, and copies of the book disappear from the school library and local bookstore—young readers enjoy it so much they move on to *Stuart Little* and *Trompet of the Swan* on their own, eventually discovering Judy Blume, and the pleasure reading habit is established. Second, being read to allows children to become familiar with the special grammar and style of the written language before they can read themselves, which may facilitate reading development and hence writing development (Smith, 1982; pp. 190–191).

[11] It is not yet clear how much "reader-sensitivity" can be taught or encouraged. Bracewell, Scardamalia and Bereither (1978; cited in Flower, 1981) report that specifying an audience more precisely improved audience-sensitivity in writers from grade four to college. Atlas (1979; cited in Flower, 1981) found that some novice writers, even when made aware of background information relevant to readers' needs still did not address these needs.

[12] Teachers and students often desire in-class one-hour-one-essay assignments because a final exam utilizes this format. In this case, however, teaching directly to the test may be counterproductive, in that it encourages a distorted view of the composing process.

[13] Our research in second language acquisition suggests that even for "good language learners", aspects of grammar beyond simple inflections are difficult to consciously learn and remember (Krashen, 1982, chapter 4). Precisely what is "learnable" for most people can be determined by error analysis and self-correction studies, using students of

different ages. Perhaps the following rule of thumb is appropriate for determining whether a rule is "straightforward" and learnable: If the teacher needs to look the rule up and study it before teaching it in class, it may be too complex!

[14] Conscious knowledge of rules of grammar and discourse may also be good therapy for some writers. Some people possess substantial subconscious knowledge but lack faith in it, feeling the need to check everything they write with a learned rule. (The same phenomenon exists in second language acquisition; see Krashen, 1981, chapter 1.) Learning rules that are already acquired may give some of these writers a greater appreciation for what they have acquired, and for the acquisition process. This may result in more confidence in their own feeling for good prose, and greater fluency.

[15] K. Birss, in an unpublished research project done for a USC linguistics course, did a survey of second language writers similar to that done by Kimberling *et al* for first language writers. International students enrolled in writing classes at USC were surveyed as to reading habits in both first and second language. Birss reported that the better writers in English as a second language reported more pleasure reading in their first language as well as their second language, with first language reading occurring in earlier years and second language reading occurring later.

[16] Brière's results do not demonstrate that output practice improves grammatical accuracy. His subjects, advanced ESL students, received comprehensible input from several sources, inside and outside of class.

Bibliography

Applebee, A. Teaching high-achievement students: A survey of the winners of the 1977 NCTE Achievement Awards in writing. *Research in the Teaching of English* 1978. **1:** 41–53.

Arnold, L. Writer's cramp and eyestrain— are they paying off? *English Journal* 1964. **53:** 10–15.

Asker, W. Does knowledge of formal grammar function? *School and Society* 1923. **27:** 109–111.

Bagley, D. A critical survey of objective estimates in the teaching of English. *British Journal of Educational Psychology* 1937. 138–154.

Bamberg, B. Composition instruction does make a difference: A comparison of the high school preparation of college freshmen in regular and remedial English classes. *Research in the Teaching of English* 1978. **12:** 47–59.

Beach, R. The effects of between-draft teacher evaluation versus student self-evaluation on high school students' revising of rough drafts. *Research in the Teaching of English* 1979. **13:** 111–119.

Birdwell, L. Revising strategies in twelfth grade students' transactional writing. *Research in Teaching of English* 1980. **14:** 197–222.

Brière, E. Quality versus quantity in second language composition. *Language Learning* 1966. **16:** 141–151.

Chomsky, N. *Aspects of the Theory of Syntax* Cambridge: MIT Press. 1965.

Clark, J. A four-year study of freshman English. *English Journal* 1935. **24:** 403–410.

Christiansen, M. Tripling writing and omitting readings in freshman English: An experiment. *College Composition and Communication* 1965. **16:** 122–124.

Crystal, D. and Davy, D. *Investigating English Style* London: Longmans. 1969.

Cummins, J. The role of primary language development in promoting educational success for language minority students. *Schooling and Language Minority Students: A Theoretical Framework* Office of Bilingual Bicultural Education (Eds.) 1981. Los Angeles: Evaluation, Dissemination and Assessment Center, California State University. pp. 3–49.

De Vries, T. Reading, writing frequency and expository writing. *Reading Improvement* 1970. **7:** 14–19.

Donalson, K. Variables distinguishing between effective and ineffective writers in the tenth grade. *Journal of Experimental Education* 1967. **4:** 37–41.

Dressel, P., Schmid, J., and Kincaid, G. The effect of writing frequency upon essay-type writing proficiency at the college level. *Journal of Educational Research* 1952. **46:** 285–293.

Dulay, H. and Burt, M. Remarks on creativity in language and acquisition. In M. Burt and H. Dulay (Eds.), *Viewpoints on English as a Second Language,* New York: Regents. 1977. pp. 95–126.

Dulay, H., Burt, M., and Krashen, S. *Language Two* New York: Oxford University Press. 1982.

Elley, W., Barham, I., Lamb, H., and Wyllie, M. The role of grammar in a secondary school curriculum. *Research in the Teaching of English* 1976. **10:** 5–21.

Emig, J. The composing process: A review of the literature. In W. R. Winterowd (Ed.), *Contemporary Rhetoric: Conceptual Background with Readings* New York: Harcourt Brace Jovanovich. 1975. pp. 49–70.

Evanechk, P., Ollil, C., and Armstrong, R. An investigation of the relationship between children's performance in written language and their reading ability. *Research in the Teaching of English* 1974. **8**: 315–326.

Fader, D. *Hooked on Books* New York: Berkeley Books. 1976.

Faigley, L. and Witte, S. Analyzing revision. *College Composition and Communication* 1981. **32**: 400–414.

Flower, L. Writer-based prose: A cognitive basis for problems in writing. *College English* 1979. **41**: 19–37.

Flower, L. Revising writer-based prose. *Journal of Basic Writing* 1981. **3**: 62–74.

Flower, L. and Hayes, J. The cognition of discovery: Defining a rhetorical problem. *College Composition and Communication* 1980. **31**: 21–32.

Flower, L. and Hayes, J. A cognitive process theory of writing. *College Composition and Communication* 1981. **32**: 365–387.

Gardner, R. and Lambert, W. *Attitudes and Motivation in Second-Language Learning* Rowley, Ma.: Newbury House. 1972.

Grobe, S. and Grobe, C. Reading skill as a correlate of writing ability in college freshmen. *Reading World* October, 1977. 50–54.

Heys, F. The theme-a-week assumption: A report of an experiment. *English Journal* 1962. **51**: 320–322.

Illo, J. From senior to freshman: A study of performance in English composition in high school and college. *Research in the Teaching of English* 1976. **10**: 127–136.

Kaplan, R. *The Anatomy of Rhetoric* 1972. Philadelphia: Center for Curriculum Development.

Keenan, E. Ochs. Why look at unplanned and planned discourse? In E. Ochs Keenan and T. Bennett (Eds.) *Discourse Across Time and Space* Southern California Occasional Papers in Linguistics, no. 5. Department of Linguistics, USC. 1977. pp. 1–41.

Krashen, S. On the acquisition of planned discourse: Written English as a second dialect. In M. Douglas (Ed.) *Claremont Reading Conference: 42nd Yearbook* Claremont, California: Claremont Graduate School. 1978. pp. 173–185.

Krashen, S. *Second Language Acquisition and Second Language Learning* Oxford: Pergamon Press. 1981.

Krashen, S. *Principles and Practice in Second Language Acquisition* New York: Pergamon Press. 1982.

Krashen, S. and Terrell, T. *The Natural Approach: Language Acquisition in the Classroom* San Francisco: Alemany Press. 1983.

Lokke, V. and Wykoff, G. "Double writing" in freshman composition—an experiment. *School and Society* 1948. **68**: 437–439.

Mathews, E., Larsen, R., and Butler, G. Experimental investigation of the relation between reading training and achievement in college composition classes. *Journal of Educational Research* 1945. **38**: 499–505.

Mavrogenes, N. and Padak, N. The reading road to writing. *Journal of Educational Research* 1982. **75**: 354–359.

McQueen, R., Murray, A. K., and Evans, F. Relationships between writing required in high school and English proficiency in college. *Journal of Experimental Education* 1963. **31**: 419–423.

Perl, S. The composing process of unskilled college writers. *Research in the Teaching of English* 1979. **13**: 317–339.

Pianko, S. A description of the composing process of college freshman writers. *Research in the Teaching of English* 1979. **13**: 5–22.

Potter, R. Sentence structure and prose quality: An exploratory study. In G. Tate and E. Corbett (Eds.) *Teaching High School Composition* New York: Oxford University Press. 1970. pp. 174–183.

Pringle, I. Why teach style? A review-essay. *College Composition and Communication* 1983. **34**: 91–98.

Rose, M. Rigid rules, inflexible plans, and the stifling of language: A cognitivist analysis of writer's block. *College Composition and Communication* 1980. 389–400.

Ryan, J. Family patterns of reading problems: The family that reads together. In M. Douglas (Ed.) *Claremont Reading Conference: 41st Yearbook* Claremont, California: Claremont Graduate School. 1977. pp. 159–163.

Selzer, J. The composing process of an engineer. *College Composition and Communication* 1983. **34**: 178–187.

Shaughnessy, M. *Errors and Expectations* 1977. New York: Oxford University Press.

Simmons, J. Testing the effectiveness of the one-to-one method of teaching composition. Office of Educational Programs, Los Angeles Community College District. 1979.

Sommers, N. Revision strategies of student writers and experienced adult writers. *College Composition and Communication* 1980. **31**: 378–388.

Sommers, N. Intentions and revisions. *Journal of Basic Writing* 1981. **3**: 41–49.

Smith, F. Demonstrations, engagement, and sensitivity: A revised approach to language learning. *Language Arts* 1981a. **58**: 103–122.

Smith, F. Demonstrations, engagement, and sensitivity: The choice between people and programs. *Language Arts* 1981b. **58**: 634–642.

Smith, F. *Writing and the Writer* 1982. New York: Holt Rinehart Winston.

Smith, F. Reading like a writer. *Language Arts* 1983. **60**: 558-567.

Stallard, C. An analysis of the writing behaviour of good student writers. *Research in the Teaching of English* 1974. **8**: 206–218.

Stiff, R. The effect upon student composition of particular correction techniques. *Research in the Teaching of English* 1967. **1**: 54–75.

Taylor, B. Content and written form: A two-way street. *TESOL Quarterly* 1981. **16**: 5–13.

Wall, S. and Petrovsky, A. Freshman writers and revision: Results from a survey. *Journal of Basic Writing* 1981. **3**: 109–122.

Woodward, J. and Phillips, A. Profile of the poor writer. *Research in the Teaching of English* 1967. **1**: 41–53.

Zamel, V. Writing: The process of discovering meaning. *TESOL Quarterly* 1981. **16**: 195–209.

Zamel, V. The composing processes of advanced ESL students: Six case histories. *TESOL Quarterly* 1983. **17**: 165–187.

Zeman, S. Reading comprehension and writing of second and third graders. *Reading Teacher* 1969. **23**: 144–150.